ANIMAL TRACKS

To the young, oncoming naturalist, I would say: Never forget the trail, look ever for the track in the snow; it is the priceless, unimpeachable record of the creature's life and thought, in the oldest writing known on the earth. Never forget the trail!

ERNEST THOMPSON SETON
Lives of Game Animals

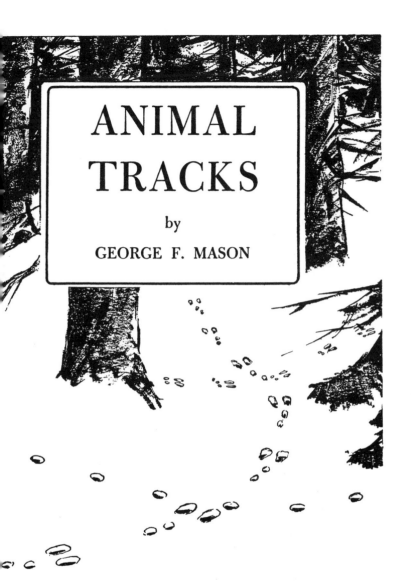

ANIMAL
TRACKS

by

GEORGE F. MASON

LINNET BOOKS
HAMDEN, CONNECTICUT
1988

Reprinted 1988 by permission as a
Linnet Book, an imprint of
The Shoe String Press, Inc.
Hamden, Connecticut 06514.

The paper in this publication meets the minimum
requirements of American National Standard for
Information Sciences—Permanence of Paper for Printed
Library Materials, ANSI Z39.48-1984. ⊚

Library of Congress Cataloging-in-Publication Data
Mason, George Frederick, 1904–
    Animal tracks.

    Reprint. Originally published: New York: W. Morrow,
1943.
    Summary: A nature guide presenting pictures of
forty-four North American animals, their tracks, and
footprints, from the whitetail deer to the jack rabbit to
the house cat. Also discusses the animal's habitat and
behavior.
    1. Animal tracks—North America—Juvenile
literature.
2. Zoology—North America—Juvenile literature.
[1. Animal tracks. 2. Zoology—North America]
I. Title.
QL768.M375   1988   599   87-31124

ISBN 0-208-02213-9

Printed in the United States of America

CONTENTS

[5]

PREFACE

This book is written primarily to aid in the identification of the tracks of our most common animals. A brief résumé of the habits and range of these animals is included for the purpose of acquainting the young naturalist with information which is educational as well as helpful.

The tracks in this book are purposely drawn to show much more detail than is generally seen in nature where tracking conditions are not always ideal. This is done with the assumption that for the purpose of identification, it is easier to compare the perfect track found in this book with the natural track which is more or less indefinite.

It is well to remember when studying tracks, that tree-climbing animals nearly always place the front feet side by side when hopping or jumping. This is called "pairing" the tracks. The tracks of animals that live on the ground seldom show the front feet paired, although the hind feet are generally paired in both tree-climbing and ground-living animals. Exceptions to these rules are observed when the animal is moving at a different gait from his normal method of locomotion.

[7]

CHIPMUNK
Tamias striatus

The CHIPMUNK in numerous species spreads over a large territory from the Arctic regions in Canada, south throughout the United States to lower California and Mexico.

The eastern chipmunks are the most familiar of our small mammals. They live on the ground where their favorite haunts are stone walls and brushy rock piles into which they scurry at the approach of danger.

Chipmunks are always alert and shy, but when fed by people for a short period, they become quite friendly. They live mainly on seeds from various grasses and plants.

When cold weather comes along in the month of October, the "Chippy" burrows down below frost line and curls up for a long sleep which lasts until sometime in March. On rare occasions he may appear on a warm winter day for a quick look around, but returns to his nest to sleep until spring.

Unlike the tracks of the tree-climbing squirrels, which are paired, the tracks of the fore feet of chipmunks are one behind the other.

On rare occasions chipmunks may climb trees, but for the most part, they remain on the ground.

LIFE SIZE

R- FRONT

R-HIND

The GRASSHOPPER MOUSE makes his home in arid, treeless sections of the west where he lives among the cacti, sagebrush and yuccas.

He occupies any hole in the ground and is not particular as to its size, using the holes of mice, squirrels, rats, prairie dogs and other animals.

This mouse has a varied diet made up of insects and meat, but he has a fierce desire for flesh and will eat parts of any animal he may find dead, as well as the small rodents he kills. The grasshopper mouse is so named because grasshoppers make up a large part of his food.

The tracks are often seen in the sand and on the snow in winter. The placing of one foot in front of the other indicates that this mouse is not a tree climber. When the track is very clear, such as might be seen when made in very fine dust, a small thumb-like impression shows on the inside of each footprint.

RUNNING
IN SAND

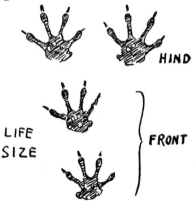

HIND

LIFE
SIZE

} FRONT

GRASSHOPPER MOUSE
Onychomys leucogaster

FIELD MOUSE
Microtus pennsylvanicus

The FIELD MOUSE, sometimes called meadow mouse, is found all over the United States (except in the arid desert regions), and as far north as the tundra beyond the tree line. They prefer the meadows and cultivated areas and any grassy sections of the woods.

Field mice are the prey of a variety of animals, such as bears, bobcats, coyotes, foxes, and hawks, but in spite of all these natural enemies, they remain plentiful, as they are extremely prolific. These little animals are a nuisance to farmers because of the amount of grain and fruit which they eat or destroy, and in winter they often gnaw the bark from fruit trees, causing great loss.

The presence of meadow mice is easily detected by the myriads of tiny runways that lead in all directions from their burrows. These trails afford a certain amount of protection since they are under a network of surface material, making tunnel-like routes over which they travel without detection.

MPING

Field mice are active in winter and their tracks may be seen on the snow. The absence of the tail mark and the fact that the front feet seldom pair distinguishes their trail from that of other kinds of mice.

LIFE SIZE

R-FRONT

R- HIND

The WOODCHUCK is familiar to all country dwellers in eastern Canada and the United States. His home is a burrow which he digs under stone walls, ledges and frequently in the open fields and pastures.

Woodchucks are a nuisance to the farmer whose vegetable gardens they occasionally ravage, and because they dig up the fields and trample the grass. Consequently, the sport of woodchuck hunting is encouraged in most farm sections.

They spend most of their time eating during the warm summer months, but when cold weather arrives, they retire to the depths of their burrows and sleep throughout the winter.

The old fable about "Groundhog Day" has given the woodchuck a great deal of prominence, and I can remember when I was a boy spending a long and chilly February day beside a woodchuck hole waiting for him to appear and look over the weather situation. He never showed up, so I lost faith in the legend of "Groundhog Day."

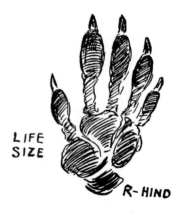

WALKIN

R- FRONT

LIFE
SIZE

R- HIND

WOODCHUCK
Marmota monax

BROWN RAT
Rattus norvegicus

BROWN RATS, sometimes known as the wharf rats or sewer rats, are familiar to everyone. They are found wherever there is human habitation, for they live on the filth and garbage that, unfortunately, are associated with civilization. Rats live in barns, storehouses, and many dwellings where the cellar walls have not been rat-proofed. They also inhabit all manner of water front structures and sewers.

Brown rats have a mental alertness and cleverness developed from their long association with mankind. These qualifications, plus a fierce and aggressive nature, enable them to hold their own in the battle for existence.

This rat is a great menace as a carrier of many dread diseases, such as bubonic plague, scarlet fever, typhoid fever, diphtheria and trichinosis.

The tracks are distinguished by the small four-fingered, handlike print of the front foot and the long heel impression of the back foot. The tail mark is always conspicuous.

PPING

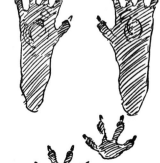

LIFE
SIZE

KANGAROO RATS are found in the desert regions of the western United States and Mexico, from Nebraska to the Gulf Coast of Texas, west to the Pacific Coast, and southward through lower California to the Valley of Mexico.

Kangaroo rats are nocturnal and they live in burrows dug in sandy soil. The large species, common in New Mexico and Arizona, live in colonies, digging up huge mounds of earth about the entrances to their burrows. Well-worn trails lead out from these mounds.

When angry or frightened, kangaroo rats make a thumping noise by striking their rear feet sharply against the ground. They are rather pugnacious individuals and often engage in impromptu bouts with one another. They strike a powerful blow with the rear foot which is sufficient to knock over a rival rat if he is hit squarely.

The small paired tracks are typical of the kangaroo rat as they use only the rear feet when bounding along or hopping about during a fight. If the animal is moving about slowly, the unpaired front footprints show.

JUMPI.

R-HIND
LIFE SIZE

KANGAROO RAT
Dipodomys spectabilis

DEER MOUSE
Peromyscus leucopus

The DEER MOUSE, or white-footed mouse as it is sometimes called, is found over most of North America from the northern tree line, south to Yucatan. They are active throughout the year and where snow falls one will always see their delicate tracks in the woods.

Deer mice sometimes live in and about cabins where they build nests and rear their young. A friend once showed me a deer mouse nest that he found in his hunting lodge in the Adirondacks. It was very cleverly built in the end of a dish mop, the tassel ends of which the mouse had chewed and torn into a silky mass, interwoven with feathers from a stuffed grouse that was on the wall of the cabin. Their nests are often found in hollow logs and in knot holes high up in trees. Where there are no trees, they live in burrows.

The pairing of the front feet indicates that the deer mouse is a tree-climbing animal. The tail mark is always present when the tracks are in soft snow. The tracks of mice and other small rodents are seldom seen except in sand or snow.

JMPING
SNOW

HIND

FRONT

LIFE SIZE

PACK RAT
Neotoma cinerea

The PACK RAT is found in the mountainous sections of the western United States and Canada.

This animal gets his name from his habit of "packing" or carrying off all manner of strange objects that appeal to his fancy. Frequently he will leave some object in place of the one he removes. The name "trade rat," by which he is known in some localities, is undoubtedly due to this curious habit. Prospectors tell of being annoyed by pack rats about their cabins, for they run off with such irreplaceable objects as magnifying glasses and eye glasses.

Pack rats occasionally migrate to new areas, probably instinctively rather than for lack of food. Their tracks are similar to those of the common brown rat, but they have more of a tendency to pair the front feet, probably due to the fact that these rats are expert climbers. The heel print is absent in the tracks of the rear feet when the animal is hurrying, but it may show when he is ambling along.

OING

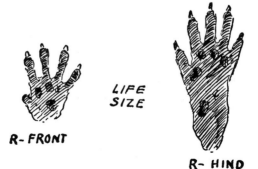

R- FRONT

LIFE SIZE

R- HIND

GRAY SQUIRREL
Sciurus carolinensis

The range of the GRAY SQUIRREL is limited to the eastern United States and southern Canada, from Nova Scotia to Florida. Years ago they were so plentiful that they were a menace to the crops of the early settlers. At one time a bounty was put on their heads in an effort to curb their plundering. Today gray squirrels are not so plentiful, being protected and much appreciated as pampered pets in many of our city parks. When captured, young gray squirrels can be tamed.

The gray squirrel is clever at hiding himself by flattening his body against a limb high in the tree tops where he hopes to evade the eyes of the dog or cat that frightens him.

Occasionally you may see a mass of dry leaves and twigs high up in the branches of a tree. This is the gray squirrel's summer nest. In winter he lives in hollow trees and stumps.

The tracks are familiar to most everyone as squirrels are so common.

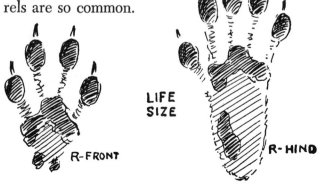

NDING

LIFE
SIZE

R-FRONT

R-HIND

The RED SQUIRREL ranges from Alaska and Canada south to Idaho, Wyoming, the Dakotas, Wisconsin, through the northeastern states to the District of Columbia, and from the Alleghenies to South Carolina.

Red squirrels prefer to live in coniferous forests where the cones of the various evergreens make up a good part of their diet.

The chattering of these squirrels can be a nuisance. Often when a hunter is stealthily approaching a game animal, a red squirrel will warn the whole country-side by his vociferous chattering which sounds like swearing, name calling, and oral lambasting. He will climb down to the low branches of a spruce tree and keeping just out of reach, proceed to voice his opinion of hunters in terms that, to my imagination, always seem very uncomplimentary.

The winter woods are almost always crisscrossed with tracks of this busy little animal, usually leading from tree to tree, as the red squirrel spends most of his time in and about

RUNN

trees. He often lives in an outside nest, made of bark strips and roots.

LIFE SIZE

R- FRONT

R- HIND

RED SQUIRREL
Sciurus hudsonicus

COTTONTAIL RABBIT
Sylvilagus floridanus

The range of the COTTONTAIL RABBIT is from the Atlantic to the Pacific and from the southern border of Canada to South America.

Rabbits are so common in the United States that every boy and girl is familiar with them. They live in any bushy growth that will afford protection, and at night they are most active, frequently coming out and feeding on the lawns of residences close to city limits. Often they may be seen at night by the glare of headlights.

In summer the cottontail uses a series of resting places or "forms" that are usually in a sheltered spot which affords protection from wind and rain, but during severe winter weather the cottontail allows himself to be buried by the drifting snow and assumes a drowsy sleep until the weather clears and he can burrow out of his storm cellar.

There is little chance of confusion in recognizing the cottontail track. In the deep swamp areas where both cottontail and snowshoe rabbits are found, the tracks are easily distinguished from one another by the smaller size of the cottontail's footprint.

FRONT

LIFE SIZE

HIND

The JACK RABBIT is typically a western animal, living in the treeless areas from western Missouri and eastern Texas to the Pacific Coast, and from South Dakota to the tableland of Mexico and the peninsula of Lower California.

In spite of having such enemies as the wolf, coyote, fox, rattlesnake, eagle, hawk and owl, jack rabbits are able to hold their own. At times, they become so plentiful that they are a pest.

When startled, the jack rabbit is apt to make one or two very high leaps, or "sky-hops," before settling down to a steady lope. It is presumed that the sky-hop is made for the purpose of getting a better view of the enemy so that the course of flight will be in the right direction.

The jack rabbit does not build a nest for its young, but places its newly born young in various "forms" and visits each one separately.

The jack rabbit track is somewhat like that of the cottontail except that the rear feet are seldom paired.

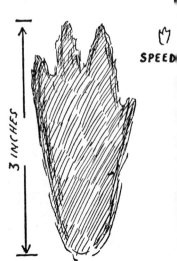

3 INCHES

SPEED

JACK RABBIT
Lepus californicus

SNOWSHOE RABBIT

Lepus americanus

The SNOWSHOE RABBIT, sometimes called the varying hare, ranges from eastern Canada and Maine west to the Pacific Coast, from the tree limits of North America, south to the northern border of the United States, down the Alleghenies to West Virginia and down the Rocky Mountains to New Mexico, as well as in parts of the Sierra Nevada Mountains in California.

Snowshoe rabbits are important in the north as a source of food for both man and beast. When they are plentiful, the trappers are sure of a good catch of lynx and fox, but about every seven years they seem to die off. With the loss of their chief food supply the lynx and fox suffer accordingly.

Because the varying hare will not hole up when pursued, it is great sport to hunt him with beagle hounds.

The hare is often seen resting in a natural "form" made under the low branches of the northern spruce.

The tracks are unmistakable, because of their great size and width.

R-FRONT

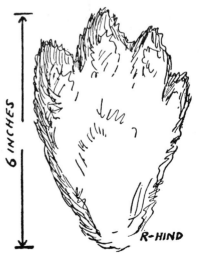

6 INCHES

R-HIND

MUSKRAT
Fiber zibethicus

The MUSKRAT is one of the most numerous and highly valued fur bearers in North America. Being extremely prolific, muskrats remain plentiful throughout their range in spite of the millions trapped each year. They occupy the territory from beyond the northern limit of trees in the Arctic, south throughout Canada and the United States.

Muskrats are aquatic, living in marshes and around ponds, lakes and streams. Their peculiar flattened tail is used when swimming and gives them far greater speed than they could make with the feet alone. The familiar piles of roots, mud and plant stems that constitute the winter homes of the muskrats are seen in many swamps in the eastern United States. Entrances to dens are always below water level, so the inhabitants may come and go unobserved.

Muskrat tracks are recognized by the drag of the knifelike tail which shows clearly in soft mud.

LIFE SIZE

R-FRONT

R-HIND

BEAVER
Castor canadensis

The BEAVER'S range extends from the mouth of the Yukon in Alaska, throughout Canada, south to the delta of the Colorado, and to the lower Rio Grande.

The beaver cuts down trees, builds dams and mud houses with a skill that wins the admiration of those who have observed his accomplishments. He is clever enough to cut his winter food supply and store it under water near his home which is a dome-shaped affair made of logs and mud. The beaver shows his ingenuity by not sealing the entire roof with mud so that fresh air can penetrate to the interior.

Beaver tracks are distinctive because of the webbed hind foot, and close examination of a good print will reveal the absence of a claw mark on the second inside toe, caused by a peculiar development of a split nail that is called a combing claw.

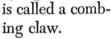

ING
ING
DRAG

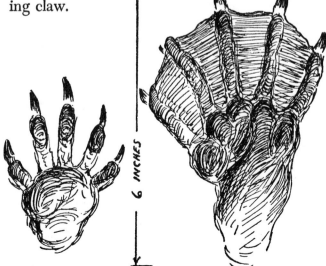

6 INCHES

The FISHER is a forest animal and has a wide range over the United States and Canada.

Although he has been exterminated from the southern border of his range, the fisher is still found in the forest areas of New York, Vermont, New Hampshire and Maine, west to the Great Lakes region and along the Rocky Mountains to Wyoming, in Canada from the southern shores of Hudson Bay throughout most of eastern Canada.

The fisher is more agile than a squirrel in running through the tree tops, and can run down the very elusive marten.

Porcupines are often killed and eaten by fishers. To avoid the sharp quills, the fisher flops the porcupine over on his back so that the underparts are exposed.

If you find a fresh fisher track the chances are that he is still on the move and will not show up again in that vicinity for some time, since he covers a large territory in his wanderings and generally returns at intervals of several days or weeks.

BOUND

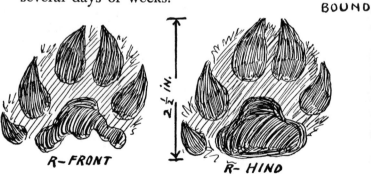

R-FRONT   R-HIND

2½ IN.

FISHER

Mustela pennanti

WEASEL
Mustela noveboracensis

The WEASEL is one of the most widely distributed animals, being found from the most northerly polar regions of North America, south to South America.

The northern variety turn from brown to white in winter but, in regions where there is no snow, this change does not occur.

Weasels are bold and bloodthirsty killers. They will kill for the sheer lust of killing, as well as for food. They do not seem to fear the presence of man, and often make their abode under a trapper's cabin or the outbuildings on a farm.

The extraordinary vitality of the weasel is almost unbelievable. One of them invaded my camp in the mountains of British Columbia, drawn no doubt by the smell of blood from a freshly killed sheep. He dodged in and around a pile of saddle-bags and pack mantles until I finally frightened him away.

When running, the weasel often leaves only two prints at each bound instead of four. This is due to the hind paws landing in the tracks made by the fore paws.

BOUNDING

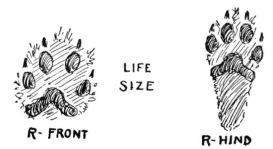

LIFE SIZE

R- FRONT

R- HIND

MARTEN
Martes americana

The North American MARTEN ranges over the wooded areas of Alaska, Canada, and parts of the Rocky Mountains and the Sierras. He is extremely shy and keeps to the wildest sections of the pine and fir forests where few people, except trappers, venture. Although an abundance of tracks may indicate that martens are present in an area, few men can boast that they have ever seen one alive in his natural habitat.

When caught alive, martens are easily tamed and the young born in captivity make excellent pets.

The marten is a relentless hunter with flashing speed and tireless vigor. His victims include mink, squirrels, rabbits, mice and birds as well as frogs, fish and some insects. His den is usually built in a hollow tree.

When following a marten trail, the resemblance of the track to that of the weasel is quite evident. The larger size of the marten track distinguishes it from the latter.

MPING

R-FRONT

LIFE
SIZE

R-HIND

MINK
Mustela vison

The North American MINK is found all over the northern part of the continent and throughout the greater part of the United States, as far south as the Gulf Coast. It is not present in the arid southwestern states.

Mink are courageous fighters and will kill animals much larger than themselves for food. Their boldness is shown in the story of a mink which my grandfather told me. He was in the woods when he heard a rabbit squealing, and upon investigating saw a mink in the act of killing a snowshoe rabbit. Walking up to the animals he picked up the dead rabbit and was surprised to observe that the mink ran round him in circles, eyeing the rabbit with bloodthirsty anticipation. Hanging the rabbit from a tree out of the mink's reach, he went home to get a gun and on returning he found the mink still running about under the dead rabbit.

Although the mink has five toes on each foot, only four toes show in the track. The tail mark is often present when the trail is in deep snow.

BOUNDING

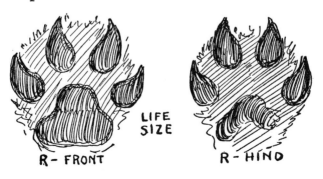

LIFE SIZE

R - FRONT　　　R - HIND

SHORT-TAILED SHREW
Blarina brevicauda

The range of the SHORT-TAILED SHREW is eastern North America. They live in damp woody sections where they burrow shallow tunnels similar to those of the field mouse. They are active throughout the winter and networks of tunnels may be seen just below the surface of the snow where they burrow for long distances in search of food. When cold weather begins, shrews will often gather near barns where food is more readily found.

They are omnivorous, but probably prefer a carnivorous diet which is made up of mice, earthworms, young birds, snails, slugs and many kinds of insects. Shrews prefer the type of food found in and about rotted logs and stumps and surface vegetation.

Their tiny eyes are of little use except to distinguish light from dark.

Shrews are fierce fighters and will not hesitate to attack mice much larger than themselves and when annoyed they make a squeaking noise that can be heard for some distance.

During the winter, shrews burrow about under the snow in search of food, and their tracks may be seen occasionally on the snow.

The tail mark is prominent in their trail either when walking or hopping.

WALKING

SPEEDING IN SNOW

BADGER
Taxidea taxus

The BADGER ranges from about latitude 58° in Canada south to the Mexican tableland. It was formerly plentiful in many of the western states but today its numbers have been greatly reduced.

Badgers like dry, loose soil and are not found in swampy or rocky country. This preference is due, no doubt, to their digging ability which is developed far beyond that of other larger animals. Badgers are so slow-footed that they invariably depend on digging to catch whatever small animal they may find "holed up."

Badgers are ferocious and will fight when cornered. Being extremely strong they can give a good account of themselves when the odds are not too great.

Badger tracks can be seen in the soft earth around the numerous holes that they dig. The long sharp claw marks are always conspicuous.

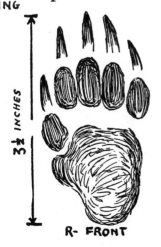

WALKING

$3\frac{1}{2}$ INCHES

R- FRONT

R- HIND

The OTTER ranges from the Arctic barrens of Alaska and Canada, south throughout the United States and parts of Mexico and Central America. He lives in the vicinity of rivers and streams but often takes long jaunts overland from one stream to another, even though his short legs are not adapted to land travel. In water he is graceful and extremely swift, being able to catch fish on which he depends for the greater part of his food.

Otters are very playful, showing particular delight in sliding down smooth river banks on their stomachs. This sliding habit is noticeable when following the trail of an otter in the snow. He seems to depend on the force of a leap to propel his body over the snow or ice like a toboggan.

Otters have their dens in the river bank where the entrance is under water. The exit leads to the surface of the bank and serves as an air vent as well as a passage from the den.

RUNNING

TA
OR

JUMPI

R—FRONT

3 INCHES

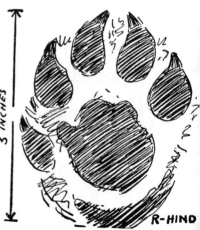

R—HIND

OTTER
Lutra canadensis

OPOSSUM
Didelphis virginiana

The OPOSSUM occupies the swampy and wooded areas of the eastern United States, particularly the warmer southern states. He is fond of water and is most plentiful around wet lowlands and swamps. His den is in any kind of hole.

Opossums eat almost anything, either animal or vegetable. Their feet are adapted to climbing, so they are often found on the limbs of fruit trees, especially the persimmon trees in the south.

The expression "playing 'possum" no doubt comes from the opossum's habit of playing dead when he is molested.

The tracks are easily distinguished by the peculiar pads on the bottom of the feet and the development of the thumb which makes it possible for him to grasp limbs when climbing. He depends on the grip of the toes and tail, as well as the claws.

This toe grip is used when the young opossums cling to the fur on the mother's back, where they ride as she moves about.

LKING

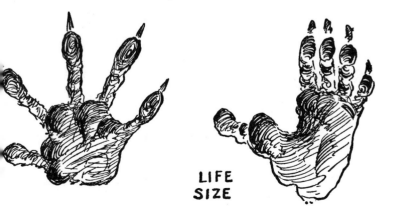

LIFE
SIZE

The SKUNK is probably one of the best known animals in North America. They range from Great Slave Lake and Hudson Bay in Canada, south throughout the United States and Mexico as far as Guatemala. Through this vast range, skunks are found in all types of localities with the exception of heavily wooded forests and arid desert plains. Their den is in any available hole that is dry and warm.

They are fond of insects as well as rodents, frogs, snakes and birds.

As in most cases with animals that dig, the skunk is a clumsy walker and when frightened into running, he goes into a peculiar gallop that is anything but graceful. He walks on the soles of his feet instead of the toes, so that the track looks a lot like a miniature bear track. The claws on the fore feet are well developed and always show in the track, but the hind feet seldom show any claw marks.

WALKING

GALLOP

L- FRONT

LIFE SIZE

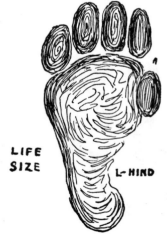

L- HIND

SKUNK
Mephitis mephitis

RACCOON
Procyon lotor

RACCOONS are found in the wooded areas over most of the United States and as far south as Panama. In this country they are most plentiful in the southeastern states.

Although they are expert tree climbers, they spend most of their lives on the ground, particularly around water. This fondness for water may be due to their peculiar habit of washing their food. The raccoon's den is invariably located in a hollow tree.

Their diet consists of fresh water clams, frogs, crawfish, birds and their eggs, fruits and green corn. "Coon" tracks are easy to distinguish because the hind feet rest flat on the ground and the print looks like the track of a small child. The front feet have long slender toes and are used like hands when they pick up food and other objects.

You will find raccoon tracks in the sand and mud along streams and lake shores. Sometimes they may be seen in the soft earth in a cornfield.

R- FRONT

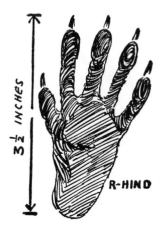

$3\frac{1}{2}$ INCHES

R-HIND

The North American PORCUPINE is a woodland animal, living for the most part in the coniferous forests of the north.

They originally were present in all forested areas of the continent as far south as West Virginia and Texas, but with the disappearance of the forests, they have retreated to the timberlands in more northern areas.

Porcupines live on bark and twigs of spruce, hemlock, pine and cottonwood trees, as well as various vegetables. They are particularly fond of salt.

Porcupine tracks are rarely seen except in snow or along the muddy bank of a pond. They are distinctive in their short, waddling gait and the tendency to toe in. The porcupine is so short legged that if the snow is very deep he plows a furrow with his body as he walks.

WALKI

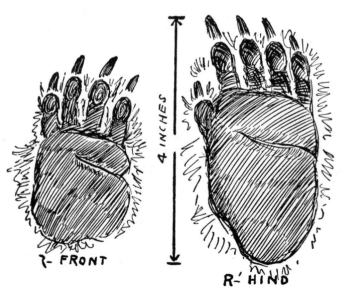

4 INCHES

R- FRONT

R- HIND

PORCUPINE
Erethizon dorsatum

DOG
canis familiaris

DOG tracks are so common that it would seem unnecessary to include them in our list of animal tracks. But we have done so in order that the naturalist may have a comparison for the tracks of the wolf, coyote and fox.

It is almost impossible to distinguish a wolf or coyote track from that of a dog, although the larger foot of the wolf helps to identify him from most normal-sized dogs. The fox track differs from the dog's in three easily noted characteristics: the pads are much smaller and surrounded by tufts of fur; secondly, the fox foot is longer and narrower; and thirdly, the fox trail is unique in that the tracks are all in a single line.

The dog tracks shown here are those of the beagle hound who often roams the winter woods following rabbit trails. Setters and spaniels have tufts of hair about the toe-pads similar to the fox's, but the dog has larger toe-pads although the foot may be the same size as the fox's.

LK

TROT

GALLOP

WOLF
Canis mexicanus

The WOLF, before the white man settled in North America, ranged almost the entire continent with the exception of southwestern United States and southern Mexico. Today wolves are plentiful in western Canada and Alaska, and occasionally one is found in our western states.

When trying to determine if the trail you are studying is that of a wolf or a dog, it is helpful to notice the locality and character of the country through which the trail leads. A wolf is most likely to take advantage of every bit of cover, while a dog ranges over open country, disregarding the protection of brush and woods.

The track of a wolf is not unlike that of a large dog, although it is usually larger than that of the average dog. I measured a wolf track in Rainy Pass, Alaska, and was amazed at its extraordinary size. The track measured five and a half inches long by four inches wide. This was no doubt the track of a very large wolf.

LKING

LOPE

HALF
LIFE SIZE

RED FOX
Vulpes fulva

The RED FOX ranges over nearly all the forested area of North America. His food consists of mice, birds, reptiles, and, if convenient, he will raid the poultry yard.

Foxes are active all winter, and their tracks are easily distinguished from those of a dog by the size of the pads, which are much smaller, and by their habit of placing one foot directly in front of the other.

It is interesting to follow the trail of a fox when the snow is a few inches deep. You will find the story of his eating habits as you follow the single-line track through the woods and fields. Here he ambushed a cottontail and ate him, hair and all; here he dug out a mouse. Next we see where he stalked a grouse but the grouse got away by flying up into a tree. Farther on the trail leads to a sheltered spot where the fox curled up for an afternoon snooze.

If there is a stump or rock that offers a vantage point the trail will often lead to that, as foxes like to jump onto such places. They can stand on their back legs when they want to look over tall brush or grass.

BOUNDING

KING

RIGHT HIND

LIFE SIZE

The WOLVERINE is found in the northern part of this continent. He formerly ranged from the tree limits of Alaska and Canada, south to the northern United States, as well as down the Rocky Mountains to Colorado and parts of the Sierra Nevada range. As a consequence of his value as a fur bearer and his general nuisance to the trapper, the wolverine has been greatly reduced and is extinct over much of his former territory.

The wolverine is a savage and powerful animal about whom the northern trappers tell many varied and marvelous tales. No food cache or trapped animal is safe from destruction if this animal is in the vicinity.

The tracks of a wolverine look somewhat like a wolf track when they are made in mud or light snow, but in deep snow the squat body plows a furrow that makes identification very definite. The fifth toe shows faintly when tracking conditions are ideal.

WALK

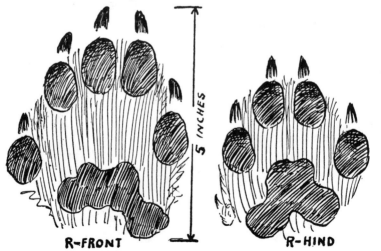

5 INCHES

R-FRONT

R-HIND

WOLVERINE
Gulo luscus

COYOTE
Canis mearnsi

The COYOTE ranges from parts of Alaska, down through Alberta, British Columbia and the western United States, south to Costa Rica.

A smaller species of the coyote known as the Arizona coyote (*canis mearnsi*) inhabits the arid deserts on both sides of the lower Colorado River and southwestern Arizona.

Coyotes are adaptable to extreme cold as well as to the hot arid desert regions; this, along with their extraordinary fecundity, keeps them plentiful over the greatest part of their original range.

To those who frequent the open plains of the west or the wilds of British Columbia, the coyote is a source of interest and amusement. Their high pitched yapping can be heard almost any night, and often during the day they will come quite close to camp and sit down in a spot where they can view the surrounding country.

The coyote tracks look quite like a dog track.

RUNNING

LKING

LIFE SIZE

The MOOSE is found in the forest areas of the north. The largest species inhabit the Kenai Peninsula in Alaska. The range of the moose runs from the mouth of the Yukon River in Alaska and the lower Mackenzie southward to Maine, northern Minnesota and down the Rocky Mountains to Wyoming.

In summer the moose live in the vicinity of the lakes, swamps and streams. In the fall when their antlers are grown, the bulls wander into the higher country to seek out a mate, for this is the breeding season. At this time tracks may readily be found, as both cows and bulls are roaming about.

The tracks of a full grown moose are larger, longer and more pointed than those of any other hoofed wild animal. Where there are moose you will find "wallows" which are shallow pits about three feet in diameter and from six inches to one foot deep. These are pawed out by the bulls and good impressions of their footprints can often be found in them.

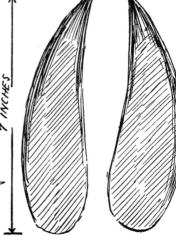

7 INCHES

WALK

MOOSE WALLOW

MOOSE
Alces americanus

WAPITI, commonly called elk, originally ranged over a greater part of the northern United States and some parts of Canada, but are found today only in western Canada, Montana, Wyoming, Colorado and the Pacific Coast states.

Wapiti spend the greater part of their lives in high forested areas, but winter snows force them to lower country where often it is necessary to feed them to prevent them from starving to death.

During the mating season the bulls are heard bugling as they round up the cows. At this time the bulls are dangerous to approach and will charge at any provocation.

The tracks of the bull can be distinguished from those of the cow by the bluntness and usual toeing out of the bull. The space between the toes is greater in a cow. Often the footprints of older and younger elk are equal in measurement. The size of the larger animals can be determined by the width of the space between the right and left footprints.

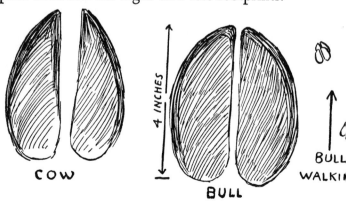

COW

4 INCHES

BULL

COW
WALKI

BULL
WALKI

WAPITI

Cervus canadensis

The WHITETAIL DEER is the well known deer of the swamp and forest areas in eastern North America. It ranges from northern Ontario to Florida, and from the Atlantic Coast to the western plains.

A light snowfall of about two or three inches is the ideal condition for tracking deer, and you will not have to go very far into the woods to find deer tracks, for the whitetail seems to thrive close to civilization. In summer, you may occasionally find deer tracks in the mud along the edge of small ponds and lakes, or around a salt lick.

The footprint varies in size according to the age of the deer. The track of a full-grown buck is about three inches in length, while the doe track is about two and a half inches, and is slimmer in appearance. The fawn makes a track about an inch long.

When a deer is bounding at full speed, the hoofs spread much more than when the animal is walking, and the clouts leave their mark if the snow is deep enough.

WALKING

BOUNDING

WHITETAIL DOE
LIFE SIZE

WHITETAIL DEER
Odocoileus virginianus

GOAT
Oreamnus montanus

The ROCKY MOUNTAIN GOAT lives on the rugged slopes and rocky ledges of the mountains from the head of Cook Inlet, Alaska, southeast to Montana and Washington.

The goat is a rugged animal and can exist through the winter gales on high peaks where few beasts care to venture. He is dangerous to approach when wounded, and can inflict a terrible wound with his rapier-like horns.

The hoofs of the goat are marvelously constructed to suit his needs. They have large cushioned areas which act like suction cups, enabling him to climb over precipitous rocky slopes where no other man or beast could possibly go.

Since goats spend most of their lives on rocky mountains, their footprints are rarely seen except in snow or the moist earth of their trails.

Although he is indifferent to wind and cold the goat does not like rain which he avoids by going into caves or under sheltering cliffs.

WALKING

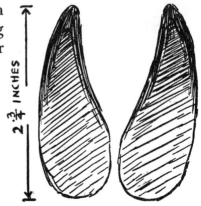

2¾ INCHES

ROCKY MT. SHEEP
Ovis canadensis

ROCKY MOUNTAIN SHEEP occupy the main range of the Rocky Mountains from the Peace River of British Columbia south to Colorado.

Mountain lion, lynx, wolf, wolverine and eagle prey on sheep, but in spite of all of these they hold their own in the ranges that are not hunted too frequently by man.

The ability of mountain sheep to leap from crag to crag and dash down the steep shale slopes is marvelous to see and even the lambs seem to be born with the surefootedness of the parent. Like the Rocky Mountain goat, sheep depend on caves for protection from bad weather. Sheep and goats are the only horned animals who use caves for this purpose.

The tracks are frequently observed in the packed earth of a sheep trail and of course in winter when they come down to lower levels they may be seen in snow. In identifying the sheep track, the slight hollow in the outer edge of each hoof is a characteristic worth noting, as well as the stubbiness of the toes.

LKING

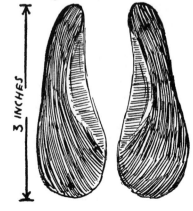

3 INCHES

PRONGHORN ANTELOPE were, years ago, almost as plentiful as the bison, and records of early explorers mention seeing vast herds of antelope on the western plains.

They are distinctly adapted to the open plains of the west and they do not live well in captivity, or on a limited range.

The rump patch of the antelope is made up of long, stiff white hairs which are raised or lowered according to the animal's will. The sun reflects on this patch of white, enabling one to see them from a great distance.

Another peculiarity is the shedding of their horns every fall and the growing of new ones over the remaining core.

The pronghorn is a very swift runner and can outdistance most of his natural enemies, but like so many of our wild animals he is rapidly diminishing before the onslaught of civilization. Fortunately, there are now strict laws which protect the antelope.

The tracks are quite wedge-shaped, distinguishing them from deer tracks.

WALKIN

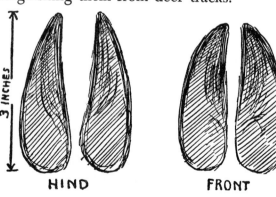

3 INCHES

HIND   **FRONT**

ANTELOPE
Antilocapra americana

PECCARY
Pecari angulatus

The COLLARED PECCARY is limited to the southern parts of Texas, New Mexico and Arizona, south to Patagonia. In the tropics, peccaries live in the thickly wooded areas and dense jungles, but in the southern parts of the United States, they make their home among the cactus plants of the plains.

Peccaries travel in bands of from five to twenty-five or more, each band having a leader. Large bands of these little animals are said to be dangerous, since the entire tribe will fight if any one of the individuals is harmed.

Their food consists of roots, nuts, fruit, grubs, reptiles and rodents. They root up the soil in much the same manner as the domestic pig.

The jaguar is their most feared enemy in the tropical jungles, but farther north, wild cats and coyotes prey on the young.

LKING

The tracks have the same characteristics as those made by the barnyard pig.

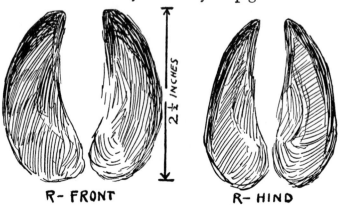

R- FRONT   R- HIND

HOUSE CAT
Felis domestica

"Enough snow to track a CAT" is an old expression often heard in New England after a light snowfall. Snow covers the details of the ground with a clean white blanket and when the family cat returns from his nocturnal prowl, he leaves clear-cut evidence in the freshly fallen snow.

The young naturalist can learn a good lesson in tracking by trailing the family cat and observing the prints under various conditions. If you study cat tracks, it will help you to recognize and understand the tracks of other members of the cat family such as the mountain lion, lynx and bobcat. The tracks of these wild animals are different in size, but their character is similar.

The tracks are ideal in a half inch of snow and again when the wet feet go over a dry, flat surface, but on sand and loose soil they become more difficult to make out.

The best formed and most permanent footprints of a cat that I ever saw were in the cement on a sidewalk in New York City. Tabby had chosen the proper moment to walk over the freshly laid cement, and thus left a lasting record.

WALKING

GALLOP

LIFE
SIZE

LYNX
Lynx canadensis

There are two types of **LYNX** in North America: the Canada lynx which is the large, beautiful animal with tufted ears and long ruff, ranging from Alaska and the tree limits of northern Canada to the northern border of the United States; and the southern variety called the Bay lynx which is smaller and less colorful in appearance, ranging throughout wooded areas of this country.

The curiosity of this animal was demonstrated to me once when I was hunting snowshoe rabbits in Alaska. I became separated from my hunting companion and circled to try to locate his tracks in the snow. I eventually crossed my own trail and was surprised to find the fresh tracks of a lynx right on my trail. He evidently was following me all the time, but I never caught sight of him.

In winter, the feet of lynx are so heavily furred that the track in snow looks quite round and there is no visible mark of the toe-pads.

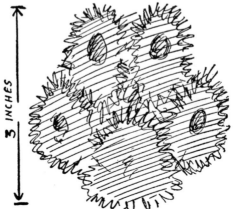

WALKING
IN
SNOW

3 INCHES

BOBCAT
Lynx ruffus

The BOBCAT, sometimes called wild cat or bay lynx, ranges over the wooded and bushy areas of most of the United States. He is smaller than the Canada lynx and less heavily furred. The ears show some tufts but less conspicuously.

There are endless "wild cat" stories in the hunting lore of America, which always make good reading, but the bobcat is only dangerous when cornered and will not attack humans without provocation.

Bobcats do their hunting and prowling at night and will come out of the wilderness to roam about the outbuildings of back country farms. If not properly protected, young lambs and poultry will fall victims to this nocturnal prowler.

The tracks are similar to a house cat's, but much larger. The bay lynx does not grow a heavy fur over the toe-pads in winter as does the Canada lynx.

The wild cat makes its den in hollow trees, with an entrance a few feet from the ground. The nest is lined with leaves or moss.

LIFE
SIZE

The MOUNTAIN LION is the largest of the cat family in North America. Years ago he roamed over both North and South America from coast to coast, but today he is found only in some of the western states and Central and South America.

When all the game has been killed off in a locality, the mountain lion must move to new territory. The presence of the lion indicates that game is fairly plentiful.

He will prey on young cattle and colts to such an extent that a large bounty has been placed on his head. He is destructive to the deer population in any district he roams.

The lion track is very much like that of a common house cat, only enlarged several times. A full grown lion makes a footprint from four to five inches long and about as many wide. As in most animal tracks, the rear footprint is slightly narrower.

The mountain lion's den is usually at the entrance to a rocky cave or under an overhanging ledge. Occasionally they will use a dense thicket.

WALKING

RUNNING

$\frac{1}{2}$ LIFE SIZE

MOUNTAIN LION
Felis couguar

BLACK BEAR
Ursus americanus

The range of the BLACK BEAR runs from the wooded sections of the Arctic, south throughout the United States and down the wooded Sierra Madre to Jalisco, Mexico.

There are several races of the black bear included in this range. There is a brown phase of the black bear which is of the same species. A black bear will have both brown and black cubs.

Because they hibernate early in the winter, you seldom see their tracks in the snow, but from springtime when the bears come out of hibernation until fall, their tracks may be observed on the sand bars along rivers and in the muddy edges of lakes.

To avoid confusion between the footprints of black and grizzly bears, it is well to remember that the grizzly's long talon-like claw leaves a much longer mark than that of the stubby short claw of the black bear.

LKING

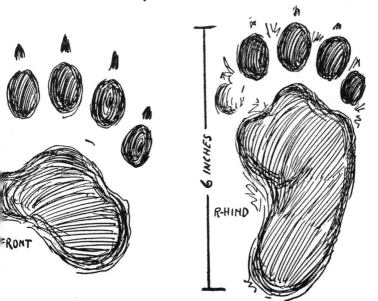

6 INCHES

R-HIND

FRONT

The GRIZZLY BEAR ranges from Alaska and western Canada south throughout the Rocky Mountains and the Sierra Madre of Mexico.

These bears are undoubtedly the source of more hair-raising tales than any other animal in North America. One man who has spent a lifetime in country where bears are plentiful told me that he never saw a grizzly that didn't turn and run when he approached. And the very next day I talked with a man in that same locality who had been attacked and badly mauled by a grizzly. The best advice one could gather was to give a grizzly a wide berth.

The tracks are enormous as compared to most wild animals. The long claw marks distinguish the grizzly from other species of bears. Occasionally, claw and teeth marks are found on trees.

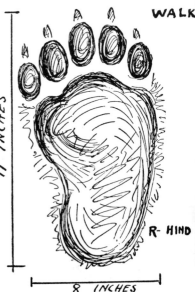

WALK

R- HIND

11 INCHES

8 INCHES

R· FRONT

GRIZZLY BEAR

Ursus horribilis